God Speaks

God Speaks

Edited by
Charles Robb

VILLARD ❦ NEW YORK

ISBN: 0-375-50427-3

Random House website address: www.atrandom.com
Printed in the United States of America on acid-free paper

2 4 6 8 9 7 5 3

FIRST EDITION

For
Nancy Fletcher,
Sheila Hayes,
and the membership of the
Outdoor Advertising Association
of America

Acknowledgments

When I look back on it, there are so many people who contributed to making this a reality, I find it hard to know where to begin. Of course, Andy Smith was a big part of it. His business acumen and support have been invaluable. My ex-wife, Mary Fran Robb, was (and is) always there as a friend and sounding board to keep the vision pure and the project on track. Then there are all the people who critiqued sections of this work and contributed opinions as well as enthusiasm: Craig and Allison, Rex, Cindy, Joan, Sunshine and Patty, Lane, Doug Mahon, Sandi Neuman, Pamela Landi, Linda Alteri, Daniel Borst, Tammy, Gecko, Kate and JD, Debbie, Ann in Toronto, Ellis Levine, Geri, Judy and Betty, Bill Duke, Candy Sullivan, Mary and Dave Balardi, John Oltman, John and Eileen Robb, Meaghan Rady, Pat Signorelli, Andy Robb, Bonnie, and Cotton. Of course, it would be unforgiveable not to mention and thank my editor at Random House, Kate Medina, whom I am totally awed by, and who saw the project the same way I did from the very beginning. Last but not least, I have to thank the one who made this all possible in the first place . . . God.

Introduction

This all started in June 1998. I was working as the creative director for the Smith Agency, a small advertising firm in Fort Lauderdale, Florida. Andy Smith, the president of the agency, came into my office one afternoon to discuss an unusual assignment from an unusual client.

The client, who wished to remain anonymous, wanted us to create a billboard campaign that would reach people who had, for whatever reason, drifted away from church or synagogue. The idea was to get people to think about their spirituality and having a relationship with God in their everyday lives.

At the time I thought it somewhat ironic that I would be asked to work on an advertising campaign designed to reach . . . well, me. Because like a lot of people, my attendance at religious services had become pretty much limited to weddings and funerals.

We didn't think that overtly religious messages would be the answer here, but rather that this campaign would have to be something contemporary yet totally unexpected. That's when I thought of creating the series of quotes in *God Speaks*.

My method was simple: As I thought of the fundamental lessons I had learned from my parents and in Sunday School, I tried to put them into the language of today, often with a sense of humor. Later, when the campaign was a success, an interviewer asked me how I knew God had a sense of humor. I said, "If he doesn't, I'm in serious trouble."

From more than one hundred lines created, we chose eighteen to run as ads in the Fort Lauderdale campaign. While those first "God Speaks" lines ran the gamut from serious to poignant to funny, all were designed to make you smile in recognition—and then think about some of the deeper levels of your life and yourself.

The look of the campaign, we believed, should be simple, straightforward, and stark. The result: black signs with white type. No logo, no phone number.

The client liked our ideas, added a couple of lines, and shelled out in the neighborhood of $150,000 for the first billboards. It still astounds me that someone could be altruistic enough to pay for something like this and not want recognition for it. I believe what he said was, "The message is what's important here, not who paid for it."

At any rate, the campaign we called "God Speaks" began running in September 1998, and the billboards were scheduled to be up for three months. Almost as soon as the ads appeared, the local press began to cover the story. It seemed as if we were doing interviews daily. Everybody wanted to know who the anonymous client was, but on that subject, we weren't talking. Soon, the story began to get national attention: Peter Jennings closed *World News Tonight* one evening with it, and CNN ran it internationally. (I know this because I got a call from a woman who saw it on TV in Israel.) There was also a segment about "God Speaks" on the *Today* show.

Three months later, just as the original billboards were coming down, the Smith Agency got a call from Eller Media, perhaps the largest billboard company in the world, saying that Mr. Eller himself had heard of the campaign and wanted it to run nationwide! He wanted to know if the anonymous client would donate the billboard sayings. The answer: In a heartbeat!

The Outdoor Advertising Association of America (OAAA), the trade group made up of all the companies who own and rent billboards, was approached by Eller, and they agreed to coordinate making "God Speaks" their national public service advertising campaign for 1999. And by the end of 1999, the campaign had appeared on something like 10,000 outdoor signs in 200 cities around the United States. It has also been translated into Spanish for Puerto Rico, and there are plans in the works to take "God Speaks" worldwide.

I've been asked why I think "God Speaks" has generated so much interest, and of course I can only speculate, starting where most writers start, with myself and the people I know. I think people today are deeply interested in getting back to the traditional values they were raised with, or in forming their own strong ties to ethics, to morality, to humanity. And within this introspective quest is a place for the kind of humor that makes self-discovery more enjoyable and life more fulfilling. That certainly is the perspective of "God Speaks."

But I think there's another reason why these "quotes" from God resonate with people. The God at the heart of this is an approachable, caring deity. He is not only a wise and forgiving friend, but rather a presence who has seen all the human foibles, who understands our trials and tribulations, yet urges us to reevaluate every day—even on the fly—our internal moral compasses. To keep the big picture in mind, to make our lives matter. And He speaks in a kind and gentle way.

So here is *God Speaks,* the book.

God Speaks

We really need
to work on
our relationship.

–God

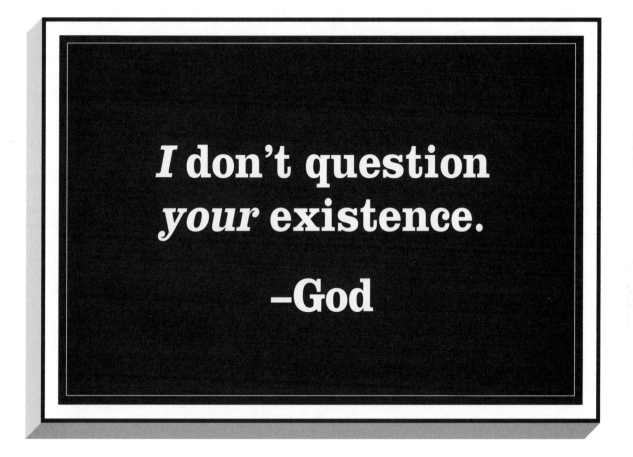

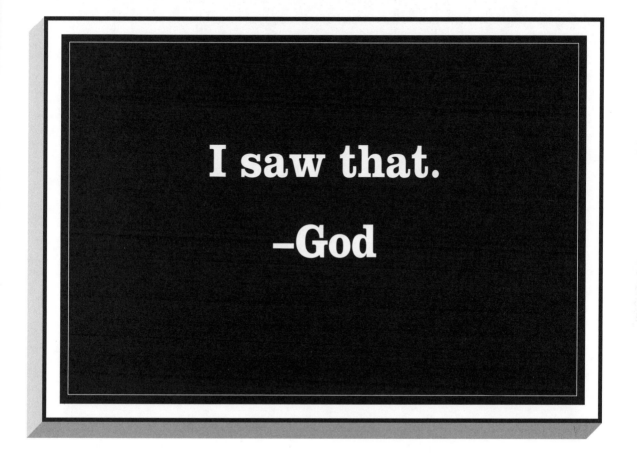

I'm also making a list and checking it twice.

–God

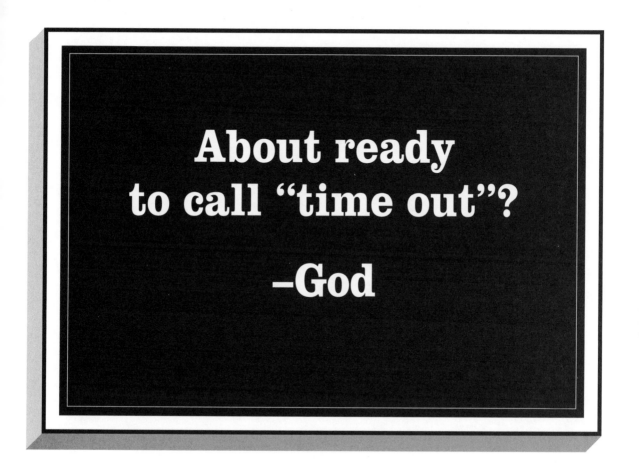

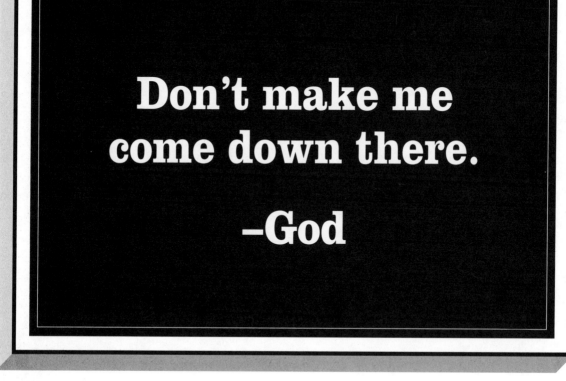

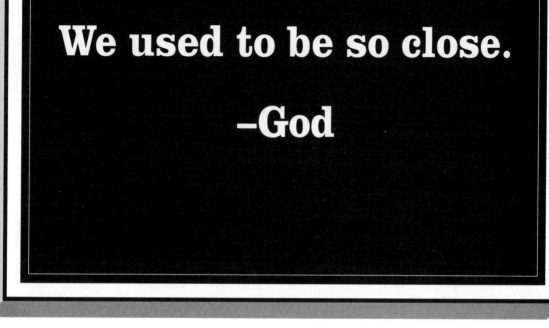

If we don't communicate, you haven't got a prayer.

–God

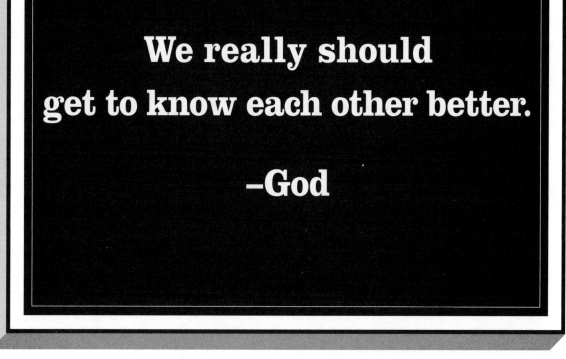

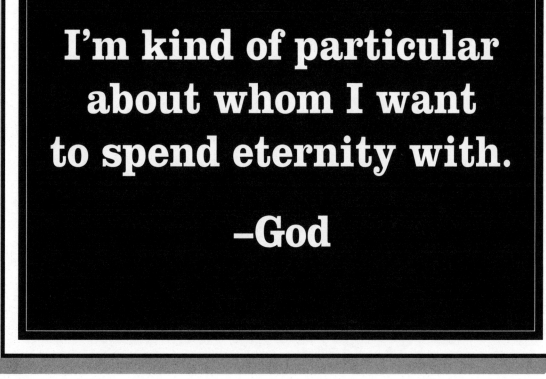

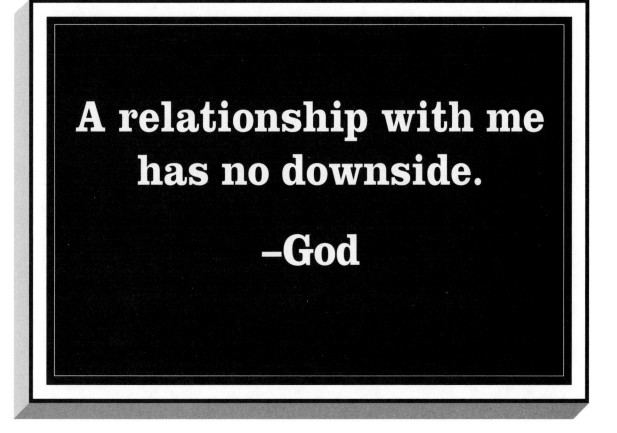

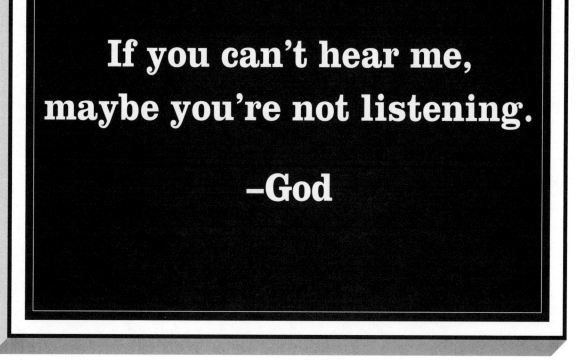

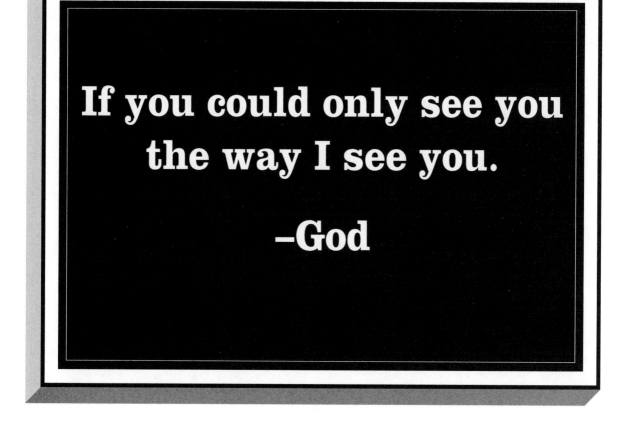

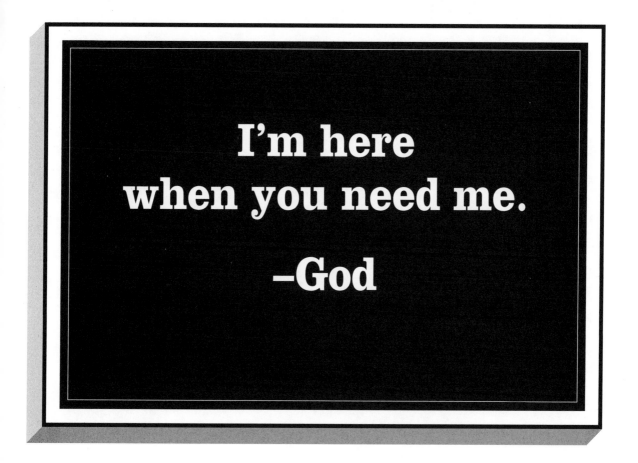

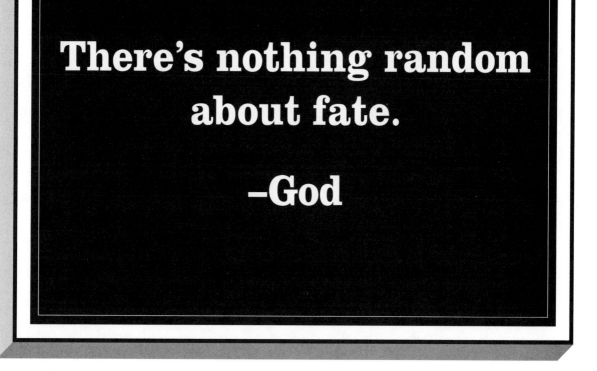

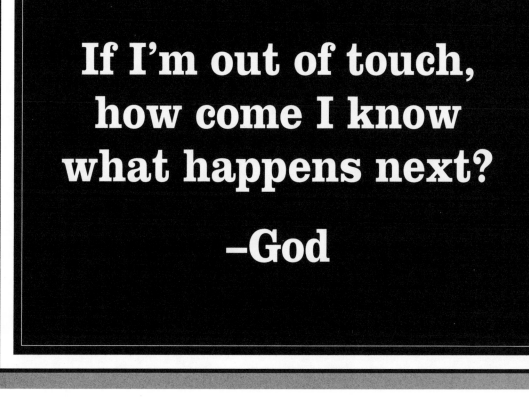

Boy, these millenniums just fly by, don't they?

–God

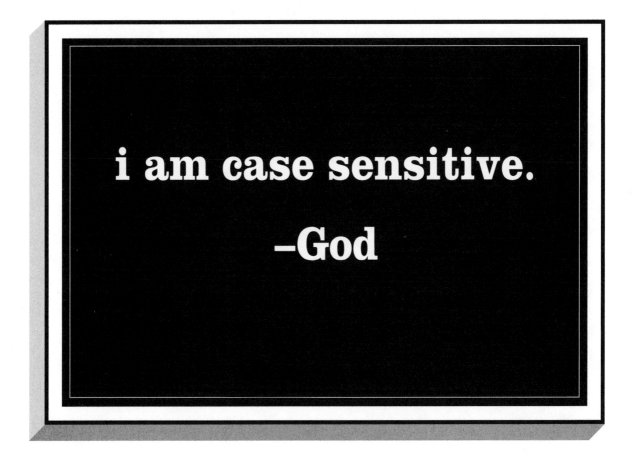

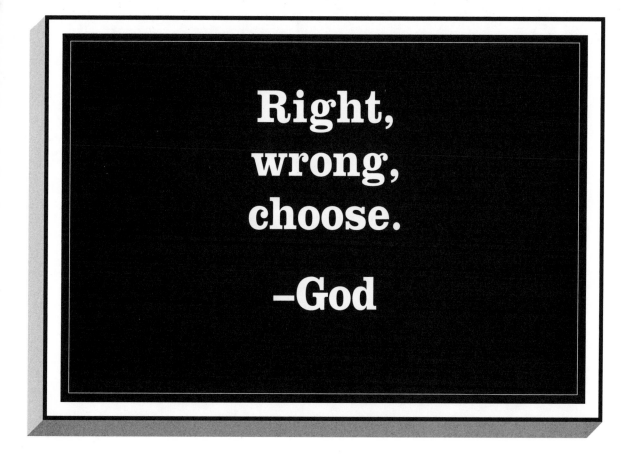

I heard your prayer;
I just don't care
who wins the game.

–God

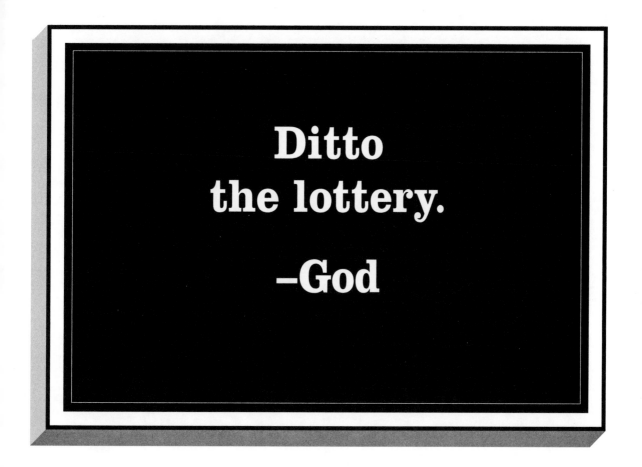

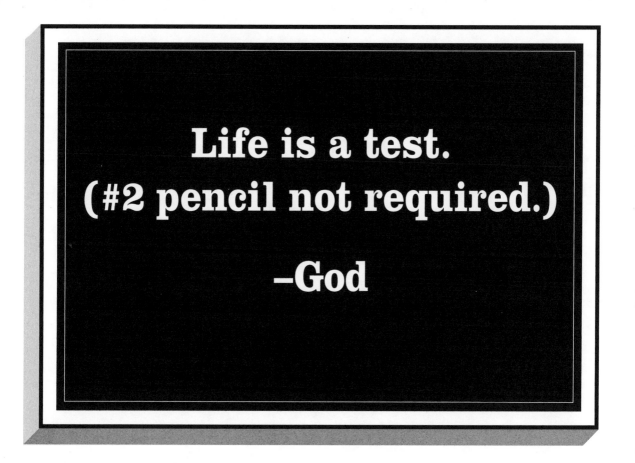

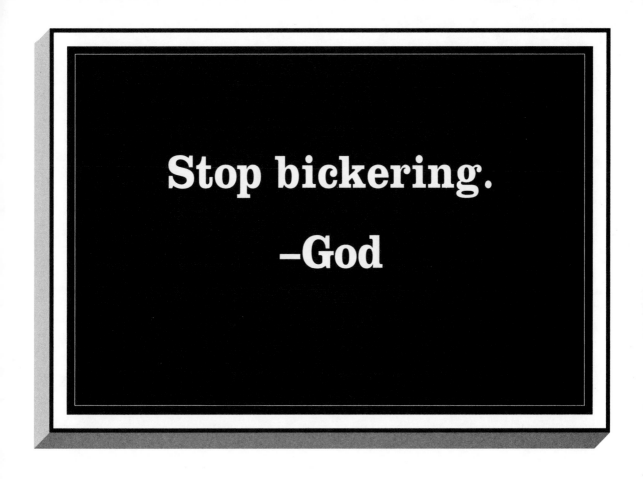

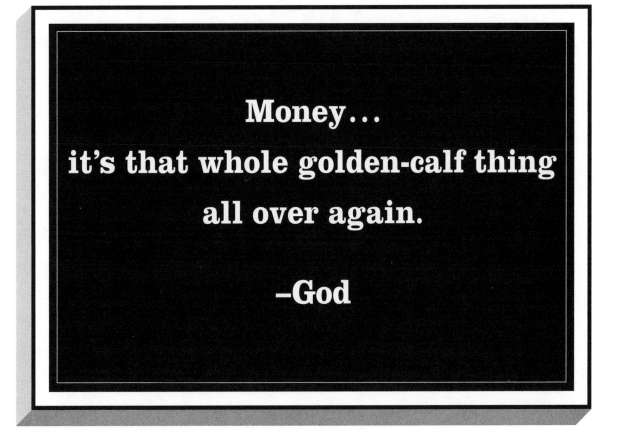

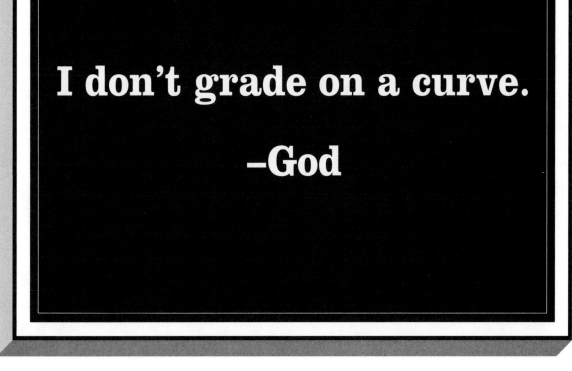

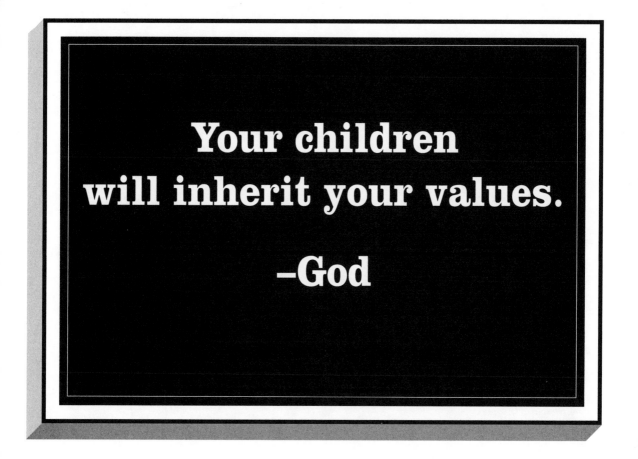

If you have to back-burner something, make it your career, not your kids.

–God

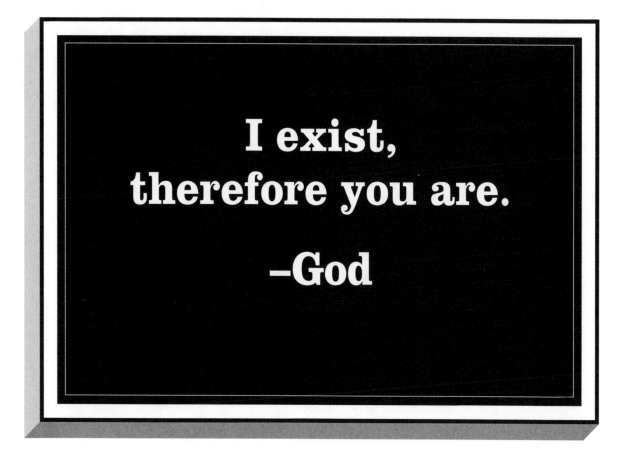

Last time
things were this messed up,
I sent a flood.

–God

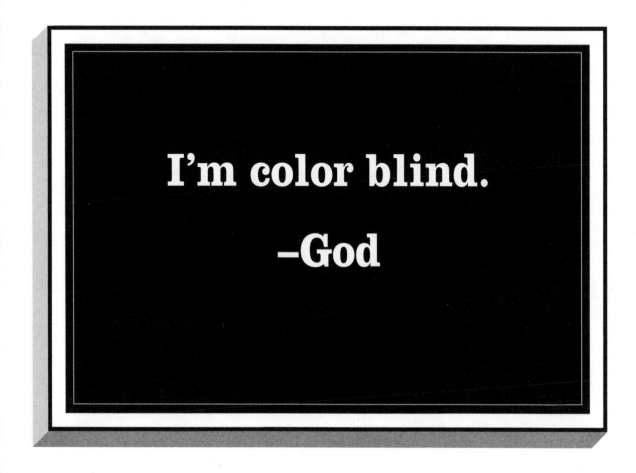

I like to think of marriage
as a bond
between just the three of us.

–God

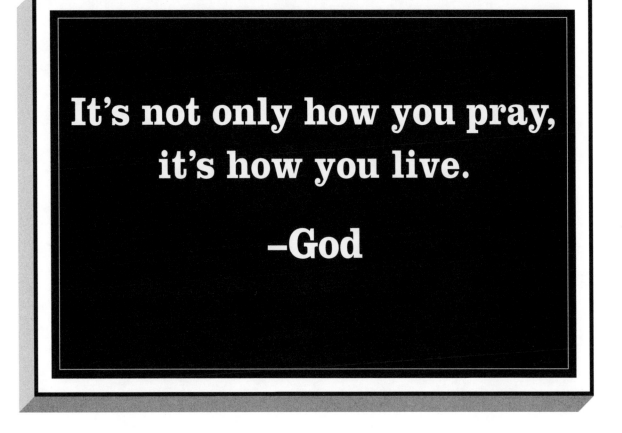

Remember how we'd talk
every night at bedtime?
I miss that.

–God

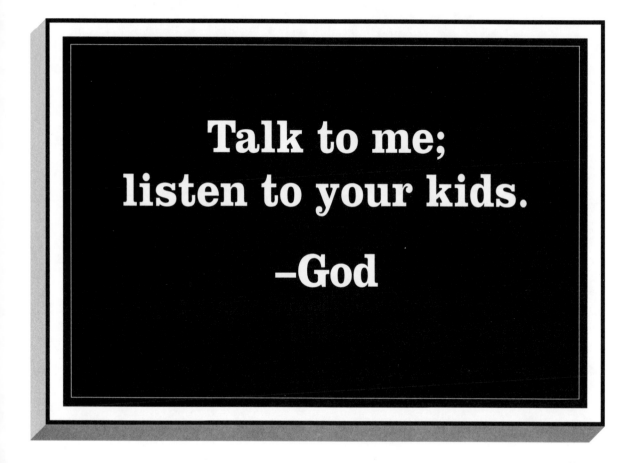

I can think of ten things that are carved in stone.

–God

**What do I have to do,
tattoo the Ten Commandments
on your heart?**

–God

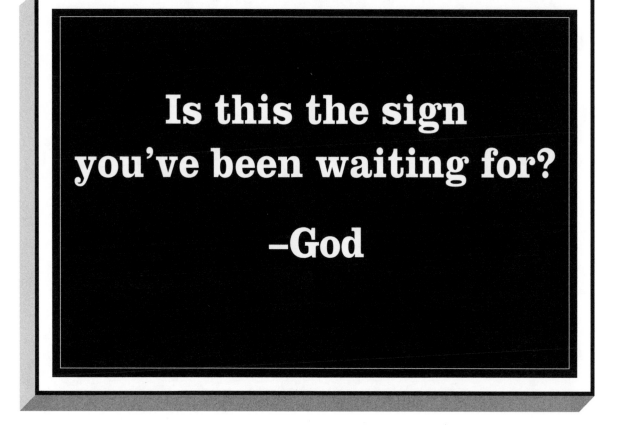

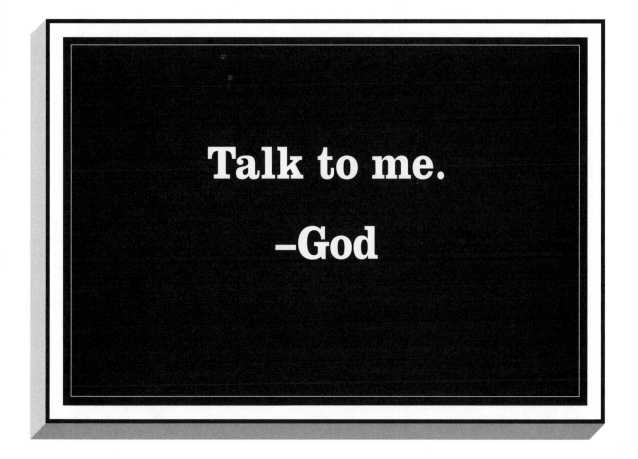

**Funny thing about kids...
you don't have to teach them
to love.**

–God

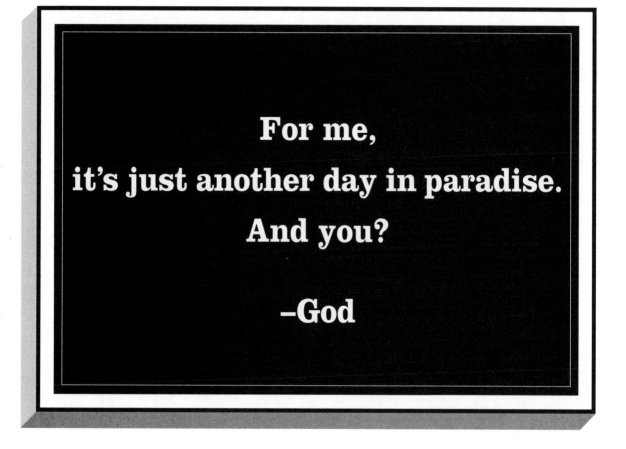

You know,
"Bless you" doesn't *have* to be preceded by a sneeze.

–God

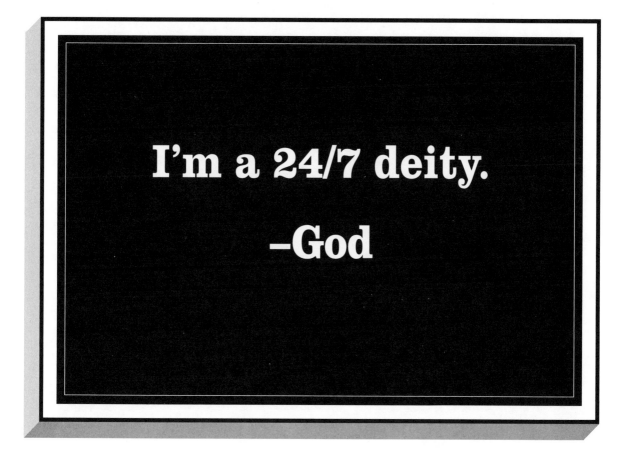

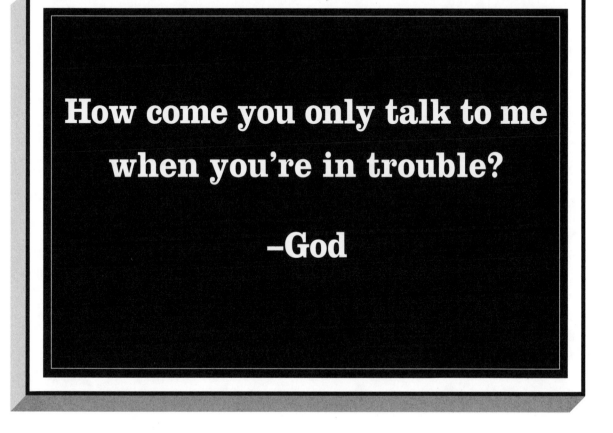

I'm a really good listener.

–God

You'd be surprised
at what
I'm willing to forget.

–God

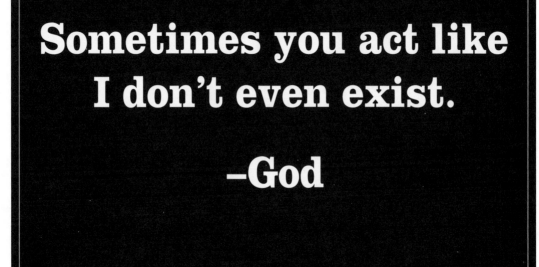

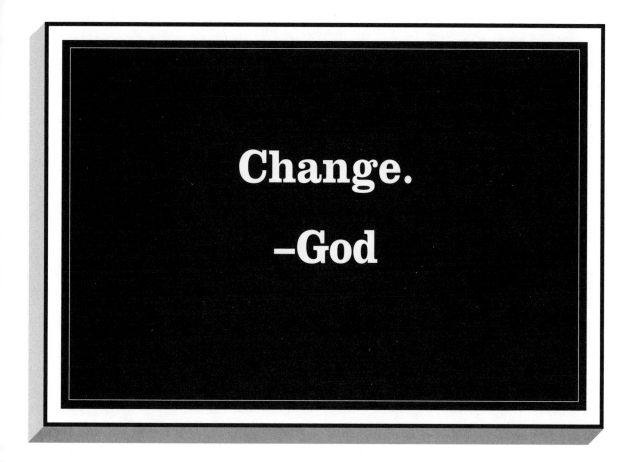

What if
you don't believe in me...
and you're wrong?

–God

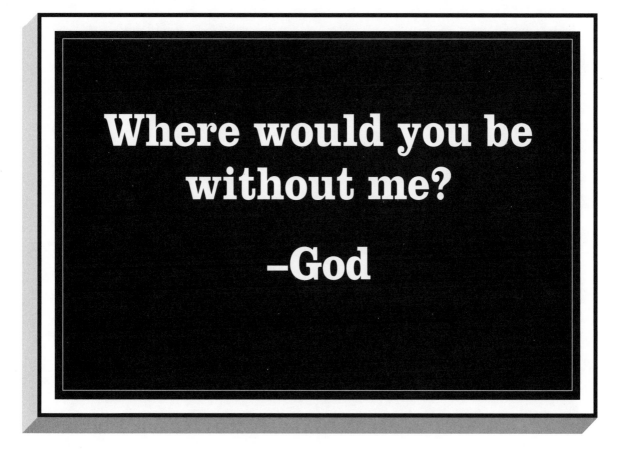

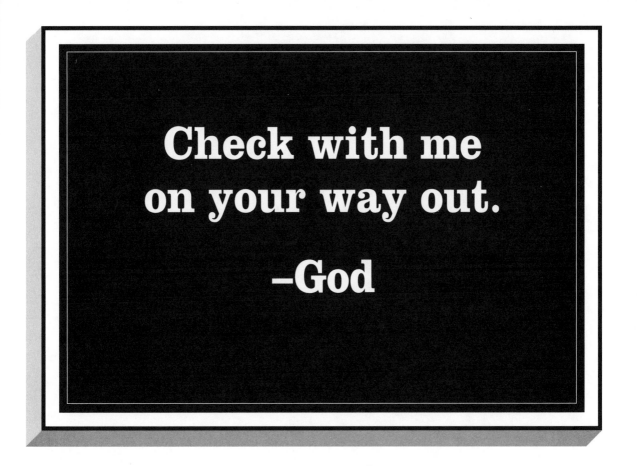

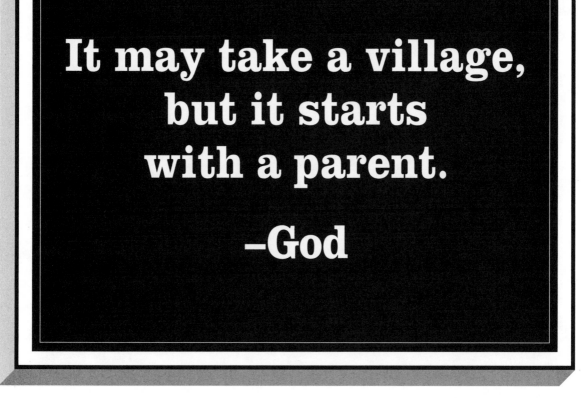

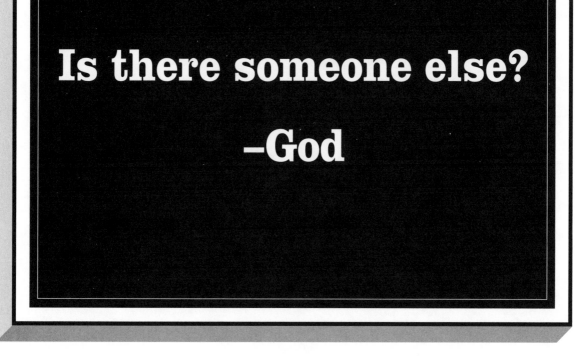

I have big plans for you.

–God

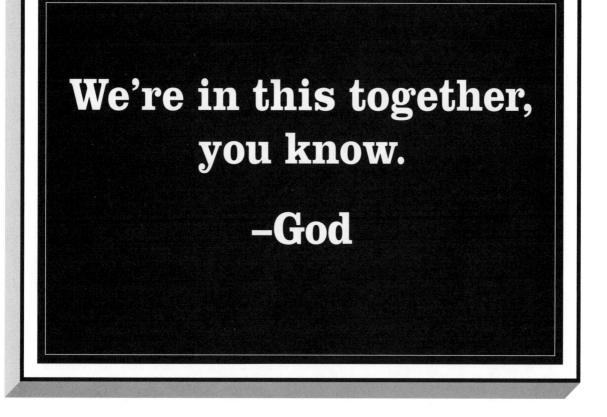

Those who preach hate aren't speaking for me.

–God

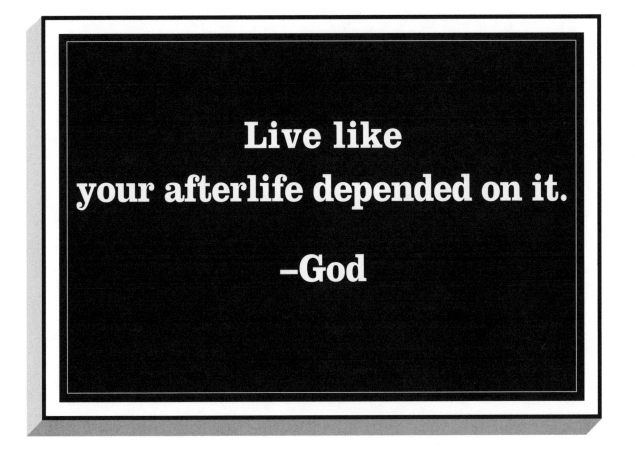

ABOUT THE AUTHOR

CHARLES ROBB has spent the past twenty years in advertising. He has won numerous national and international advertising awards for his writing, including the One Show, the New York Festivals, the Mobius Awards, and the Obies. He lives in Fort Lauderdale.